the kingdom is backwards

the kingdom experiment

A Community Practice on Intentional Living

Bruce Nuffer / Liz Perry / Rachel McPherson

the **HOUSE** studio

The House Studio, Kansas City, Missouri

The authors would especially like to thank those who gave up a great deal of their own time to help make this book what it is now, including Brent Germain, Travis Petty, Ryan Scott, and Tim Troxler.

We would also like to thank many others whose feedback and criticism helped guide us through difficult passages: Kimberly Adams, Tim Baker, George Baldwin, Emily Benson, J.R. Caines, Gary Condon, Chad Crenshaw, Jake Edwards, Mark Evilsizor, Brandon Hill, Jason McPherson, Yvonne Nuffer, Kylee Pearson, J. Paul Pepper, Leah Pepper, Bonnie Perry, Chuck Self, Jason Sivewright, Adam Spriggs, Matt Slawson, Ted Voight, and Stefanie Hendrickson.

Acknowledgments

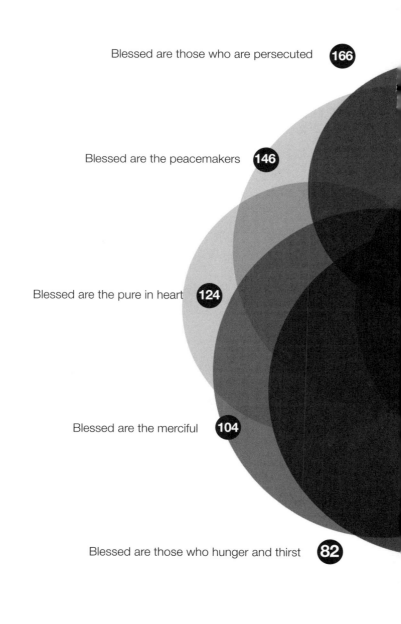

contents

most good things
have been said far
too many times
and just need to be
lived.

Shane Claiborne

So NOT an Introduction

We've gotta be honest. When we started writing a book on the Beatitudes, a few of us got nervous about the viability of the whole project. Sort of ran for the hills. Fortunately, there's nothing but flatlands here in the Midwest, so we didn't get very far before the Holy Spirit and our coworkers found us.

Mainly, we just had a lot of questions. The first? Would there be anything new to say? Anything that wasn't cliché, or hadn't been preached in a thousand sermons already?

One thing was certain, we didn't want this to end up as a "how-to" for getting blessed. We think this world has enough self-help books in Barnes and Noble to keep us more than occupied for the next century. Agreed?

So, we began brainstorming this project the only way we knew how. We sat down at a table and started talking ideals, what we personally wanted out of a small group. Bruce, the real adventurous servant, wanted a small group that was hands-on. Active in the community and such. Rachel, the deep, ministry-minded one, cared more about learning new things from the Bible and being intentional with Scripture. And Liz, the abstract art lover, just wanted to journal during the week and share thoughts with her friends.

Then it dawned on us. (We love it when this happens.)

Why can't we do them all? In one book?

Some will call it impossible. But we'll call it uncurriculum. Or better yet,

the kingdom experiment.

And he began to teach them, saying:

"Blessed are the poor in spirit, for theirs is the kingdom of heaven.

Blessed are those who mourn, for they will be comforted.

Blessed are the meek, for they will inherit the earth.

Blessed are those who hunger and thirst for righteousness, for they will be filled.

Blessed are the merciful, for they will be shown mercy.

Blessed are the pure in heart, for they will see God.

Blessed are the peacemakers, for they will be called sons of God.

Blessed are those who are persecuted because of righteousness, for theirs is the kingdom of heaven."

Matthew 5:3-10

Let's
begin
here

We know you hate directions. But you can always tear out this page and find your own way through the book.

It's plain and simple.

1 Read and discuss a chapter.

2 Each person chooses one of eight experiments to carry out . . . or make up some of your own.

3 Journal your thoughts on our pages. (Why else would we give you so much white space?)

4 Share your stories with the group next week and on thekingdomexperiment.com.

The point of *The Kingdom Experiment* is intentional living. To work things out in community. To share life and stories while we're at it. To grapple with what good news means in the context of this specific time and place.

We'd love to know that once you're done with this book it will be impossible to read the Beatitudes without understanding them as a present reality. The kingdom is here *now*. And the blessings Christ promises are just icing on the cake when we make a commitment to living his way.

And if this book helps you turn this way of living into a habit, we wouldn't complain about that either.

It's like unpacking. And boy is this suitcase big.

The eight Beatitudes are found at the beginning of Jesus' Sermon on the Mount. They aren't catchphrases or proverbs meant to stand alone . . . so don't even try the esoteric thing and Scripture-drop these on an unsuspecting brother—you know, to gain super-Christian points or something.

By opening his teaching with these counter-intuitive statements, Jesus was creating some tension that he resolved throughout the rest of the Sermon on the Mount. That's why we can—and should—draw liberally from the whole passage as a way to contextualize what the Beatitudes look like when they are lived out. It might give us a more holistic picture of kingdom living.

Things to think about:

This particular sermon mattered for some reason. Both Matthew and Luke chose to write it down, though it's believed that Jesus would have given hundreds of similar messages during his three-year ministry. Judging by its length, this was no small hand cramp.

Also, the folks who were listening would have understood the significance of *how* and *where* Jesus delivered this sermon. You see, Jesus was constantly fulfilling the prophecy of Old Testament Scriptures, which is why the Pharisees could never quite write him off.

Here's some context from where the people stood. Israel's entire existence is shaped around one epic event: their exodus out of Egypt. While in the desert, the prophet Moses climbed up a mountain and received a word from God. He called it the law, which represented ways they could please God and learn about his heart.

The chance to know this previously-abstract God got them real excited. For like a minute. And then they spent the rest of their lives breaking all the laws and trying to clean up after themselves.

Thus began a vicious cycle of elected priests who went around policing the Ten Commandments (and some of their own laws) with the belief that if all of Israel could go one day without sinning, God would come to earth in the form of a king . . . flowing robe, long gray beard, and lots of perks to pass around. Right?

Wrong.

17

Israel's attempt at perfection is unsuccessful to say the least.

Fast-forward a good thousand years, give or take some change. Now Jesus climbs up a different mountain and says he has an updated word from God. Mainly, that he is the new word. A living embodiment of God's new law.

He even proclaims, "You have heard that the law of Moses says . . . But I say" (Matt. 5:21-22).

Like we said, prophecy fulfilled. Only this isn't the kind of Savior everyone has been dreaming up.

Right away Jesus begins asking the people to repent, which really just means to rethink . . . everything. He says there is a different kingdom at hand, and that this kingdom will be counter to everything they've known. Which gets them awfully excited considering their current economic, social, and spiritual conditions are less than par. And we're talking way less. Let's just say between Caesar and the Jewish priests, it seemed pointless to even suit up.

Jesus' main intention for speaking a blessing over the disenfranchised was to assign them worth in a way no one had before. He was flipping things upside down. Establishing his kingdom in the margins. More than that, he was entering into a covenant with the people—promising to actively fulfill that declaration of blessing in their lives.

Often when we read the Beatitudes out of context, we turn them into conditional statements. *If I want God's blessing, then I better seek after persecution or petition tragedy.* But that's missing the point. These blessings aren't necessarily mandates, but rather natural manifestations of kingdom living.

There's something else we've got to know. What's the deal with the two separate, slightly differing accounts of this sermon?

Couldn't Matthew and Luke have compared notes or something? Meaning, Luke was short and to the point, always including woes that make us kind of sad. He also concentrated heavily on physical trials. Matthew, on the other hand, left out the woes and seemed to embrace spiritual trials alongside the physical kind.

Like authors these days, each had a unique purpose for his message. Something specific he was trying to get across. Matthew wanted to give people a picture of the new kingdom—the good things God was up to. Luke was more concerned with showing people the problems with the old kingdom and the things Christ came to alleviate.

Regardless of the writers' differences, the message is the same. The kingdom has come. It's *already* here because Jesus brought it with him. But it's *not yet* complete until he returns to perfect it. It's the kingdom of the *already* and the *not yet*. Which is where we live—between the tension. And it's a messy place to be.

Blessed are the poor in spirit

"Blessed are the poor in spirit, for theirs is the kingdom of heaven" (Matt 5:3).

There are a lot of poor people around us. Well, maybe not around us. Because in a day of a booming middle class and shiny plastic things that spend like money, it seems we've got to be real intentional about seeing the poor.

Regardless of our proximity to poverty, it exists. Jesus said so himself. "The poor you will always have with you" (Matt. 26:11). Even for those of us who aren't on the economic fringe, we're pretty familiar with what it looks like.

Notice that Luke's and Matthew's accounts of the Sermon on the Mount read a little differently where this verse is concerned. While Luke believed Jesus was addressing physical poverty (Luke 6:20), Matthew goes a bit more abstract on us. He supposed Jesus was also speaking to the emotional toll of poverty—to our spiritual desperation during times of trial.

Look at it this way. When our present circumstances are good, we're content to focus on what is immediately before us. But when life is without options outside of God's grace, we are forced to engage in the narrative of hope. And hope, by its very nature, has a way of bringing us into humble relationship with that which is greater than ourselves.

Jesus was saying when we get to a place of dependency we're fortunate, because it's the devout trust sustained through poverty, rather than poverty itself, which produces blessedness.

Now skip ahead to the part where Jesus explained what trust looks like in the face of poverty (Matt. 6:1-4, 19-34). Most people in the ancient world lived on the edge of death—food, clothing, and shelter were all they needed. We understand they spent most of their time worrying about these things. So for them, as well as for us, the first step in overcoming worry is to recognize that a devout trust in God is more important than our basic needs.

i want you to be concerned about your next door neighbor. do you **know** your next door neighbor?

Mother Teresa

Talk

Many people think seeing God through the eyes of the impoverished is a better and more accurate way to know him. Does actually being poor and experiencing poverty bring us closer to God?

24

In a society where we define need as the newest iPod, it is easy to overlook the fact that we are blessed to have food on our tables. Society has adopted the mentality that the basics are owed to us. How can we adjust this mentality and live a life dependent on God for even our most basic needs?

Shut your pie hole.

Fast from food as a means of making yourself aware of its physical and emotional ownership of you. Consider how important it is, then reflect on Christ's implication that life is more important than food. Consider doing this as a group, then break your fast with a community meal.

Pen, say hello to paper.

Ten items or ~~less~~ more.

Not everyone has the luxury of choosing between fettuccini alfredo and chicken parmesan. Go grocery shopping, then donate everything to the local food pantry. And don't just camp out in the canned food aisle.

Drop a line.

Don't even give me the evil eye.

The Bible describes a person who chases after wealth as having an evil eye.[1] So when Jesus speaks of a person with good eyes (Matt. 6), he is talking about someone who is generous. In this spirit, when you drive-through this week, pay for the person behind you.

Tell the page what you think.

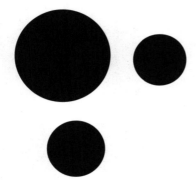

Roughing it. Air mattress not included.

Sleep on the floor for a week. Consider how life might have a different focus if this were your routine. If you're feeling extra adventurous, go without the comforts of warm water. In many places freezing showers are the norm. That's right, Brrrrrr.

White spaces are meant to be filled, says us.

I ain't no Lance.

Take your bike out (or borrow a friend's). For an errand which you would normally use your car, use the bike. Consider how your life would have to change if this were your only means of transportation. How long would you have to plan for a trip to the grocery store? How far away from home would you be able to work? What if you could only walk?

Do tell.

Go with the flow.

In her song "Names and Dates and Times," singer Ani DiFranco tells us to go to the East River and throw in something valuable, something we depend on, something we feel we can't do without. Well, don't throw it in the East River. Instead, give it away and don't replace it. Share your experience with others at thekingdomexperiment.com.

Save the ink industry. (Write things down.)

Because she's always wanted a goat.

Go to kiva.com and give a loan to someone in a developing country.

Word. (That's right, we know slang.)

Thanks but no thanks, Mr. Edison.

Minimize your use of electricity (e.g. candlelight instead of 60 watts, books instead of TV, line dry instead of tumble dry). Donate to your electric company's poverty account.

Push a pencil.

Blessed
are those
who mourn

"Blessed are those who mourn, for they will
be comforted" (Matt. 5:4).

Pretty straightforward, right? Well, maybe. Many people can attest to meeting God in some of their darkest hours. It seems that no one is exempt from the economy of give-and-take, and so we recognize the sacred seasons of both grief and comfort.

But for the Israelites, a people who were known by their exile, loss was a loaded word—spiritually, economically, and physically. Because they were always subject to foreign rule, suffering was a far more cultural and communal demonstration. We're not talking merely about observing a national holiday; we're talking about public sorrow that continued for hundreds of years.

Another way Jews would have understood mourning involved the grieving of corporate sin. Because community was so important to the Jewish identity, people understood that sin was not an isolated event.

They found it important to recognize individual participation in societal injustice. Take Joel, for instance. He was an Old Testament prophet who went to great lengths to mourn over—and repent for—Israel when the nation turned its back on God. Joel's sorrow did not manifest from his sin alone, but from the sin of his entire nation.

Sometimes we forget to carry out this part of the story—the part where the church confesses we aren't so squeaky clean, the part where saints get their hands dirty by sharing in the blame.

In our world today, as in ancient Israel, there are far too many opportunities for our hearts to be broken by the sin of others as well as our own. But that's not the final word. Christ promised to show us comfort so fully that we would then be able to turn around and comfort others (2 Cor. 1:3-4).

43

When Joel mourned
the sins of the Israelites
because he was a part
of that sinful nation,
he shared the blame.
What is the connection
between the importance
44   of true community and
mourning for the sins of
those around you?

Talk

God promises to comfort those who mourn for others and for their own sin. In what ways has God shown comfort to you or someone you know?

Decembered Grief.

Harold Ivan Smith's book *A Decembered Grief* [2] is a guide for those grieving the loss of loved ones. Get a copy. Read it so you can be sensitive to those who are mourning.

Talk to me.

Decembered
Grief

Going. Going. Gone.

Worship pastor Mike Crawford sings these words:

"Blessed when plans
that you so carefully laid
end up in the junkyard with
all the trash you made."[3]

Consider yourself and those you know who mourn the loss of a future that will never be realized. Spend a week considering how God redeems the dreams and futures of those he loves.

Self-published = write in this book.

A panoramic view.

Entire nations can lose their identity through war, exile, genocide, or poverty. Piled on top of personal loss is the loss of cultural and corporate identity. Go to tinyurl.com/cxljo8. View the University of Heidelberg's *Global Conflict Panorama*. Choose one of those areas to learn more about. Pray for those who are mourning in that situation.

Drop a line.

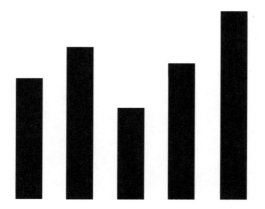

An internal war.

Those who enlist in our country's armed forces are at a high risk of depression and suicide. Provide comfort to them by sending letters, packages, or cards.

Push a pencil.

Gift shop and cafeteria. (Or you could look at it this way: shopping and fine dining.)

Attend a hospital visitation with your pastor. Feeling extra grown-up? Attend one by yourself.

Do tell.

Remember life before singing animation and e-cards?

Handwrite a letter to someone in your life who is struggling with a hopeless or depressing event.

Send it.

56

Sinners and saints.

Consider influential Christian leaders who are in the national spotlight because of their sin and have risked the faith of those they have taught. Spend a week praying for these leaders and for those whose faith has been threatened.

Pen, say hello to paper.

I just saw Abe Lincoln crying in the corner.

Ask three people what sins they feel are the most prevalent in our country. Then spend your quiet time this week interceding for our nation regarding these things.

Tell the page what you think.

Blessed are the meek

"Blessed are the meek, for they will inherit the earth" (Matt. 5:5).

He was God's chosen leader for the entire Israelite nation. He split a sea in two. He called down boat loads of plagues. He got sassy with Pharaoh. And, "Moses was very meek . . . above all the men on the face of the earth" (Num. 12:3, AMP).

Wait, what?

If we are honest with ourselves, it seems unlikely that this man would be one of the Bible's foremost examples of meekness. In fact, isn't it natural to correlate meekness with someone timid? Maybe we've got the wrong idea about this whole meek thing.

Our understanding of meek comes from the Greek word *praus*, which is used to describe a broken colt, a gentle breeze, and soothing medicine.

If you look carefully at these definitions, they all have something in common. Mainly behind the gentleness [of the colt, wind, and medicine] there is strength under control.[4] This can apply to our humanity as well. Each of us embodies a strong will which can be used in one of two ways—either to lead people toward the kingdom or drive them from it. In effect, God invites us all to become Moses to the people around us.

One more thing. When Jesus said the meek will inherit the earth, this would have created lots of hope for the people hearing his message because it conjured up memories concerning the Jewish exodus. If you remember correctly, God had made this same promise to the lowly Israelites, saying that they would inherit the earth . . . or what they called the Promised Land.

Jesus promised an inheritance for those who humbly follow God's lead. The Israelites didn't need to raise even a finger against the Egyptians when God delivered them.

True meekness is a difficult virtue to grab a hold of. It's becoming both servant and leader. It's recognizing those who are overlooked, and serving the marginalized.

Talk

Moses being "the meekest of all people on earth" may change what you have always thought of meekness. After all, he did kill an Egyptian soldier, argue with God, and smash the Ten Commandments in a fit of rage. So how does this change your interpretation of what meekness really means?

In a society constantly in pursuit of success, does meekness get in the way of succeeding? Can a person be driven and meek at the same time?

Grin and bear it, whatever that means.

Everyone may deserve to be yelled at a little—especially when they are YELLING AT YOU. But this week, when you desire to raise your voice, work to be gentle and soft-spoken instead.

Tell the page what you think.

Serving the snot-nosed.

Okay, admit it. You were a pain in the neck to all your grade school teachers. But some of those teachers still stand out in your memory as being outstanding. Write a letter to one, thanking him or her for being significant in your life. If the person is a college professor, go to ratemyprofessor.com and enter a good rating.

Talk to me.

69

While you were sleeping. (This is not a shout-out to '90s chick flicks.)

Most businesses have a night staff. Find a way to recognize their hard work. Take time to find out what kind of snack they might like, do a job or two you know is usually their responsibility, or write a letter of appreciation to both the night staff and their boss.

Save the ink industry. (Write things down.)

Why thank you, grocery-runner man.

Help people carry groceries to their cars. Or spend some time in the parking lot taking carts to the cart return for shoppers.

Word. (That's right, we know slang.)

Mow and go. (Yep, we couldn't resist the cheesy rhyme.)

Wait until they are gone, then mow your neighbor's yard. Don't let them know it was you.

Drop a line.

Still backed up on I-95.

On an unseasonably cold or warm day, take hot coffee or ice water to the crew working at a local construction site.

Tell the page what you think.

Social network pick-me-up. (Which is better than the alternative: a social network throw-you-down.)

Using your social network of choice, publicly praise someone else at least once a day. Better yet, praise someone toward whom you feel competitive or jealous.

Push a pencil.

We're giving you permission to toot your own horn.

What is your gift? Are you a brilliant carpenter? Play the piano like Mozart? Have a keen sense in finance? Whatever it is, offer your talents to help someone else—with no strings attached.

White spaces are meant to be filled, says us.

80

Blessed are those who hunger and thirst

"Blessed are those who hunger and thirst for righteousness, for they will be filled" (Matt. 5:6).

For several centuries our Western culture has been on a trajectory of affluence. Because we are able to meet most every want and need that arises, we automatically assume life owes us not only the basics, but the luxuries as well.

We're comfortable. So the concept of an urgent, life-threatening need is a little abstract for us.

But you've got to remember the Sermon on the Mount was given at a different time, to a different people. And when Jesus (being a thoughtful orator) wanted to flesh out the concept of desperation, he had to make it relevant to his audience.

Their response would have been, *Yeah, desert thirst and empty bellies for forty years. We get that.*

He's telling us to be so desperate for righteousness that our existence depends on it.

That word, righteousness, often feels too obscure to have any real meaning. That's because we have strayed away from its original understanding, which in the biblical narrative was translated more closely to *divine justice.*[5] For the Jews, empire oppression meant many were forced to give up their land and sell themselves or family members into slavery. But that wasn't supposed to be the end of the story. There was always the communal hope of things being put right. God wanted to put some skin on what righteousness looked like. And so the law stated that at the end of every 49 years, people should experience restoration. Every slave freed. All land returned. Inheritances restored. Debts forgiven.

They called this the year of Jubilee.

Yet there is no evidence that Jubilee was ever practiced in Israel, even though it was in their law. Guess they never quite brought themselves around to doing it, though the ideals were nice enough. Which begs the question, why was it so difficult for Jubilee to happen then . . . and now?

do not depend on the hope
of results. you may have
to face the fact that your
work will be apparently

worthless and even

achieve no result at all, if not
perhaps results opposite to what
you expect. as you get used to this
idea, you start more and more to
concentrate not on the results, but
on the value, the rightness, the
truth of the work itself.

Thomas Merton

What do you think the reaction would be if Jubilee became a law in the United States? Would it be well received? What problems would arise?

So we may not have Jubilee, but what are other ways to show true righteousness? How can we bring divine justice to our church? Our community?

Talk

Silence is golden. (And we've got a hunch that both silence and gold are equally rare.)

In order to pursue righteousness, some have found it necessary to remove themselves from the mainstream. Even Jesus sought retreat and solitude as a way to gather strength. Take time away. Spend a night in a monastery. Limit your external distractions so you can spend time in reflection and meditation.

Tell the page what you think.

The big Book.
Enough said.

Commit to reading the New Testament (or the whole Bible) in 90 days.
Make the journey as a group. For further direction, see
biblein90days.com.

Drop a line.

Holy Bible

Jubilee meets craigslist. (We think they're a real nice couple.)

Start a freecycling program (freecycle.org) at your church or in your neighborhood. Or set up a community where people can donate things and post needs. Donate the first items to get it started.

Push a pencil.

Doodling doesn't count, though it's pretty enough.

For one month, take notes on your pastor's sermons as a way to ensure your focus on God's Word for you. Even better, keep doing it after the first month.

Pen, say hello to paper.

Justice at town hall.

Jubilee may not exist in your hometown, but that doesn't mean you can't play an active role in the redemption of your community. Learn what issues are facing your local community council. Are there any for which you need to be present in order to speak up for divine justice?

Do tell.

I'd like some BBQ on my sorrow, please.

Righteousness is being desperate for God and depending on him. What are some other things you choose to depend on rather than God? Host a group BBQ. Allow everyone to create a list of their own obstacles to righteousness. Insert the lists into a charcoal chimney starter and use them as fuel to ignite the coals. Consider the experience a commitment to letting go of those things that we come to depend on.

Word. (That's right, we know slang.)

That cardigan is, like, so cute and slave-free.

Personal righteousness has direct relationship with social action. Ever wonder who is making your clothes? Often consumerism can lead to the slavery of factory workers in developing countries. This week, visit chainstorereaction.com and write an e-mail to stores about becoming slave-free. Further, research where your closet comes from.

Save the ink industry. (Write things down.)

Ssssshhh. Can you hear me now?

Not only can it be hard to trust in God, it can be hard to hear him because of the way we surround ourselves with noise. This week when you are alone in your car, travel in silence and consider how often our material resources—things like our car radios or televisions—keep us from listening to God.

Do tell.

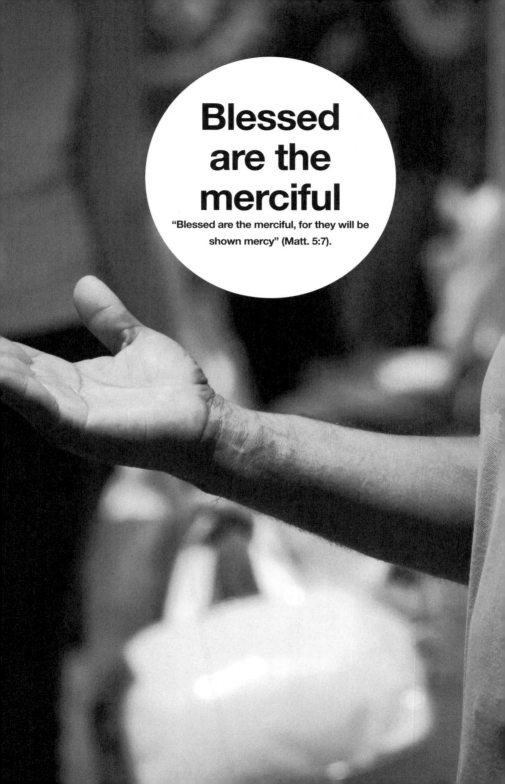

Blessed are the merciful

"Blessed are the merciful, for they will be shown mercy" (Matt. 5:7).

One way we can figure out what's important to people is to listen to what they say and notice when they repeat things. These refrains are clues to what lies in their hearts. So when Matthew tells us three times that Jesus insisted on us being merciful (see also 9:13 and 12:7), we can pretty much bank on it being core to his message.

The Jews would have immediately recognized that Matthew's comments on mercy were actually quotes from the book of Hosea: "For I desire mercy, not sacrifice" (6:6).[6] From where we stand, it sounds logical that God would prefer forgiveness over ritualistic animal slaughter. I mean, what a bloody mess. But Jesus was emphasizing something pretty huge. By suggesting that mercy was more important than giving a sacrifice—the greatest forgiveness offering in the Old Testament—he was challenging a well-established system of religion.

What it comes down to is this: God's greatest desire for us is to emulate the mercy he has shown us. But he's the polite sort, not likely to force his way on us. Rather, he invites us into an economy of mercy. The choice is ours. And if we do not feel compassion and forgiveness are the better way to live, well there's just no way we can expect to receive them. Judge and be judged.

Remember the story of the king who cancelled his servant's huge debt, only to have that servant turn around and imprison his friend over pocket change (Matt. 18:33)? Apparently he didn't get the memo.

The true disciple mimics the actions of his teacher. He is transformed when he receives mercy, making it then a natural response to demonstrate mercy toward others. That's why it's a good thing we have the perfect example of mercy in Jesus himself. It doesn't get any better than a messed up sinner being shown mercy by God. And unless our righteousness surpasses that of the Pharisees (Matt. 5:20), we need God's mercy because the good things we do will never be enough to win his favor.

Jesus says we will be blessed if we are merciful. But being merciful isn't always easy, especially with people who don't deserve it. In what situation do you find it hardest to show mercy? What makes it so difficult?

The call to be merciful can also be a challenge to those already doing good things to expand their vocabulary of righteous acts. What are some ways to expand your vocabulary?

Let the moocher live.

We all know a moocher or someone who owes us. Forgive their debt, big or small, and forget about it. And by that we mean don't tell them.

Save the ink industry. (Write things down.)

The Golden Rule just doesn't go out of style. (Unless, of course, you wear it with plaid pants.)

Think of some pet peeves you have based on what others do. Recognize that you have your own behaviors that drive others crazy. And in recognition of this fact, make accommodations for others' quirks by refusing to whine about them. Think of how you'd like others to be quiet about your faults.

Talk to me.

Hot food is overrated anyway.

We've all had waiters who forgot our drinks and then vanished for 20 minutes only to then bring out cold food. Maybe he or she was having a bad day. Give a bad restaurant server a good tip and share your story at thekingdomexperiment.com.

Word. (That's right, we know slang.)

What stop sign?

Wouldn't it be great if someone else paid for our mistakes? Exactly. Go to the courthouse cashier's line and pay someone's traffic ticket for them.

White spaces are meant to be filled, says us.

This is a hard one.

Many communities have a Web site where you can locate sex offenders who live in the area. Find out where an offender lives near your, and anonymously send that person a gift certificate to a local restaurant. Include an encouraging letter.

Self-published = write in this book.

Maybe a box. Maybe a mansion . . . doesn't matter.

It's easy to become skeptical of beggars on street corners. This month, don't think about whether they are really homeless or not, just give . . . every time. Better yet, buy gift cards to fast food restaurants or coffee shops. Keep them in your wallet and give them out.

Pen, say hello to paper.

Ugh, I *would* get stuck behind a student driver.

Hurry often short-circuits our ability to be patient. Lack of patience then leads to a lack of compassion when others force us to slow down. This week, do some spiritual training in patience—drive to and from work (or any errand) without passing anyone. And just in case you were thinking of tailgating grandma to urge her along, don't.

Tell the page what you think.

We'll call him "the frenemy." (Yeah, that's not a real word.)

Completely unaware of other people's feelings. Dominates conversation. Throws you under the bus. Can never admit to being wrong. We all have a friend who tries our patience or has betrayed our trust. Rise above the frustration. Be the friend you wish he could be, and don't resent him for who he is.

Do tell.

You've heard it before. And often.

I love you with all my heart.

You broke my heart.

Invite Jesus into your heart.

We know that no one is literally talking about the beating muscle between our rib bones. How very unsentimental. Rather, the heart is considered the core of a person's devotion, love, strength, and faith. At least that's what Hallmark says.

What's important to recognize is that when Jesus blessed those who are pure in heart, he was being kind of counter cultural.

who you couldn't touch. And yet these laws of cleanliness failed to address the most important cleansing of all—the cleansing of human will and devotion.

Jesus was doing a new thing. And it was messing with people

Blessed are the pure in heart

"Blessed are the pure in heart, for they will see God" (Matt. 5:8).

Don't get me wrong, the priests in biblical times were known for being sticklers where purity was concerned. But it just so happened that the laws of outward purity were the only ones anyone seemed to care much about. The Jews had rules addressing how many times to wash your hands in a given day, what kinds of food were pure, and

who were deeply entrenched in religious piety. In fact, the Pharisees thought Jesus embodied a sort of unreligion due to his association with the impure of society (Luke 7:34).

During the Sermon on the Mount, Christ made it clear that belief meant spiritual transformation, not just routine-following. No longer was being pure only about abstaining from murder or deception, but refraining from malicious thought as well. All of a sudden lustful thoughts were being compared to adultery.

Seems like we are set up for failure. Yet in saying all this, Jesus was pointing to the fact that people cannot, in themselves, become pure. God instead desires to do this good work in us, through relationship.

The choice to be pure in heart becomes a matter of allowing him to change us so that we can see him wherever his image resides.

he that but looketh
on a plate of
ham and eggs
to **lust** after
it hath already
committed
breakfast with it in
his heart.

C. S. Lewis

Jewish laws stated many specifics about outward cleanliness, but avoided specifics on the cleanliness of the heart. Why do you think they focused on the outward rules so much more than we do today?

Talk

Jesus says the pure in heart will see God. Assuming this does not mean a repeat of the burning bush, in what ways do you believe God shows himself to you when you strive to have a pure heart?

Media fast . . . and by that we don't mean get *faster* at flipping through channels.

Unplug from all media activity for a week as a means to simplify your life. Instead of watching that reality show, spend time seeking God. Take it one step further: reevaluate your media choices. *Gasp* Maybe there are some you should avoid or eliminate.

Word. (That's right, we know slang.)

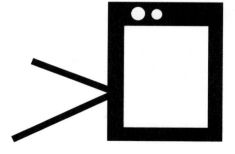

Bring a lighter.

Visit your church when nobody is there. Pray in silence for the people of your community and for the struggles and addictions of both yourself and of others. Light a candle to symbolize each person you raised up in prayer. Try tea lights.

Tell the page what you think.

For the men.

Sign up for the accountability program at xxxchurch.com. It doesn't matter if you have ever struggled with a porn addiction or not. This is a safeguard against future temptation.

Talk to me.

XXX

It's called an alarm clock. (Or the evil offspring of technology.)

Carve out space every morning to memorize Ps. 139:23-24. Pray the verses for a week (or month), asking God to reveal those areas of your life that act as a block in your relationship with him.

Drop a line.

I get by with a little help from my friends.

If you don't already have an accountability partner, seek out a trusted friend and set up times to meet regularly. Use these times to share joys, struggles, temptations, and everyday life. One of the main reasons why God created the body of Christ was so that we could encourage and support one another through this faith journey.

Save the ink industry. (Write things down.)

This will *not* be graded.

Write a letter to God as a form of confession. View this as an open communication to God as a means of mending past wrongs. Then bury it, burn it, or throw it away to signify a pure and new start.

Pen, say hello to paper.

Go green. (That is, if you're a real laggard and haven't jumped on the bandwagon yet.)

Purity doesn't stop at the physical boundaries we set for ourselves. It also involves how we treat our bodies. You may love your fast food burger, but for one week go organic. (And not because it's trendy.) If you want to go one step further, plant your own vegetable garden.

Self-published = write in this book.

I haven't had time-out since I was five.

Reflect on three of your most sacred spaces or places of retreat. Your car during a long drive. Your favorite park. That nook in your house. Visit each of these three places throughout the week to refocus on God when life gets hectic.

Save the ink industry. (Write things down.)

Blessed are the peacemakers

"Blessed are the peacemakers, for they will be called the sons of God" (Matt. 5:9).

Could be your spirit kind of recoils at the sound of conflict. Could be you have tried to act as the mediator between friends, coworkers, or siblings. That is, until you got burned. Until you stepped in between a proverbial war of words, or a not so proverbial fist fight. That's one black eye comin' up.

Could be that now you've learned some survival skills. And at the sound of slammed doors and raised voices, you retreat to a neutral corner. You still desire peace, you just stopped pursuing it. Which, more plainly put, means resigning to apathy.

When Jesus said blessed are the peacemakers, he was being intentional about his language. Notice he didn't say *peace-lovers.* He was asking us to be participants in the work of reconciliation. To leave our couches. To keep the powers of darkness from having a field day. To actively pursue peace until a new and better kingdom is realized.

Even so, waiting for such a kingdom is hard. It's easy to feel despair at the prospect of never reaching peace on a global platform, and Jesus' words aren't all that comforting. "You will hear of wars and rumors of wars, but see to it that you are not alarmed. Such things must happen, but the end is still to come" (Matt. 24:6).

It feels like we're just chasing our tails. So then, is there something to be done?

Yes. Especially if our view of peace extends beyond what we have generally thought it to be. Peace, or the Hebrew word *shalom,* indicates something more profound than just the absence of conflict (though we've never been able to achieve even that much). More appropriately, this word was used in the Bible to represent completeness or wholeness.[7] Jesus' contemporaries would have known this to include total reconciliation with God, neighbor, and nations.

Isaiah 61 mentions a whole slew of ways peace can be made— releasing prisoners, binding up broken hearts, bestowing beauty. Notice that force and fear are not the catalysts for God's shalom. So what does actively working to achieve peace look like for us today?

Would you describe yourself as more of a peace-lover, a peacemaker, or neither? What do you think caused you to be the way you are?

If peace is more than just the absence of conflict, what can we do to be active peacemakers?

Not a Grammy. Or an Oscar. But they do alright for themselves.

If you have trouble believing that peacemakers still exist, do some research on men and women who have received the Nobel Peace Prize. Pick one or two and reflect on the way they used their gifts to better our lives. How can you create peace with your talents?

Talk to me.

Bite your tongue. (Eeewww you're bleeding; that's not what we meant.)

The Scriptures say it's a pretty good idea to be "quick to listen and slow to speak" (James 1:19). But as reactionary creatures, this is hard for us. This week hold your tongue in arguments, even when you think you are in the right. Once you have listened, calmed down, and prayed about your response, then speak your mind. Be the active peacemaker in a conflict.

White spaces are meant to be filled, says us.

The Others. (Our only shout out to *Lost*, promise.)

Funny, but some of the people Christians are most at war with are those in our own faith. Denominational differences have long since been a battle between churchgoers. Arrange a joint service project between your small group and the small group of another denomination. Maybe you'll find you have more in common than you thought.

Word. (That's right, we know slang.)

Give Katie Couric a break.

It's disheartening to view national news and feel as though you are too small and remote to have any real impact. Instead, try watching the local news as a group, and consider which of the stories you could get involved in by helping the person who is the subject.

Self-published = write in this book.

Little books, big thoughts. (Okay, okay, we really just like the pictures.)

Children's author Todd Parr wrote *The Peace Book*, which happens to be a very clever and mature look at the different ways peace can be made in our world. Buy a copy at your local bookstore and pick one (or more) of the book's peace examples to focus on.

158

Push a pencil.

We actually like crayons on the wall—saves us the wallpaper hassle.

Chaos is a word most people have added to their vocabulary after having children. While endearing, children aren't known as the most peaceful of all beings. Create peace in someone's life by offering to child-sit while they go out for the night. Another option is to volunteer in your children's ministry on Sunday. Maybe some of the "regulars" would like to hear a sermon every once in a while.

Pen, say hello to paper.

The good. The badge. And the ugly.

Consider people in your town who play active roles in peacemaking: officers, teachers, civil servants, pastors. Write them a letter of affirmation, make a donation, or prepare something special to show your appreciation.

Do tell.

Zebras.

Referees are the peacemakers on the field, but seldom do they receive anything but verbal assaults. Doesn't matter if it was a ball or strike, foul or pick, first down or turnover. Keep your complaints to yourself, and personally thank the refs when the match has ended.

Save the ink industry. (Write things down.)

Jesus opened and closed his discourse on the Beatitudes by reminding us that our hope is in the age to come. But what does this mean? Based on the media's portrayal, we're ashamed to report that our picture of heaven doesn't require much in the way

Blessed are those who are persecuted

"Blessed are those who are persecuted because of righteousness, for theirs is the kingdom of heaven" (Matt. 5:10).

of imagination. Most of us are content to think that eternity exists as a refined replica of modern society, equipped with all the greats—white chocolate mochas, vacation spots, and hybrid cars. All that to say, we view heaven as an extension of earth.

Not a good thing.

At second glance, we see that things on earth are not as they were intended to be. The world feels broken. And there is no greater proof of this than the persecution of saints.

It's humbling to know that Christians continue to face hostility in many places worldwide. It happens so often that there is an entire news service—compassdirect.org—established just to report it all. However, Jesus assured his followers that their persecution and martyrdom would not be in vain: "I tell you the truth, unless a kernel of wheat falls to the ground and dies, it remains only a single seed. But if it dies, it produces many seeds" (John 12:24).

167

Christianity began in the margins and still thrives there. In fact, the areas of the world where believers receive the strongest resistance are the areas where the Church seems to be growing the most.

So why would persecution promote growth? Maybe because

the kingdom is bigger than a generic morality that people don't agree with, such as a political stance. Maybe it's more like a movement that incites others to respond. Maybe the kingdom is a real threat to the establishments, and that gets people excited. Maybe if we are living the kingdom life, our righteousness will publicly be at odds with our present culture.

Like we said, Jesus ended the Beatitudes the same way he began them: "for theirs is the kingdom of heaven." The journey has come full circle. The poor and the persecuted (and everyone in between) have something in common: they are hopeless to find solace in this present world. After all, society can't offer much in the way of comfort when we are living contrary to its patterns. And isn't that so like God, to obliterate our presuppositions and replace them with new paradigms? The Kingdom is backwards. But it is setting us free.

something is
wrong
when our lives
make sense to
unbelievers.

Francis Chan

Talk

How does living the kingdom make us at odds with the current culture? Is there any way that current culture doesn't contradict kingdom-living?

Many Christians around the world are persecuted because of their beliefs, but are there groups the Church persecutes? What groups of people does the church shun or turn away from? What can we do to reach out to these people?

Pray for the persecuted.

The Web site opendoorsusa.org has a World Watch List that continually reports which countries suffer the greatest persecution for their religious beliefs. Download the list and pray for a different area each night.

Tell the page what you think.

Voice of the Martyrs.

The Voice of the Martyrs is a nonprofit group that strives to make the world aware of the persecution Christians suffer. Go to their Web site at be-a-voice.net. Become a part of the Be-A-Voice network, then find the profile of a persecuted Christian and make a commitment to write and pray for this person.

Talk to me.

You have 346,918 Facebook friends. (Give or take a few.)

But not everyone is a social whiz. In your church there are people who are lonely—outcasts either by intentional or unintentional exclusion. Find someone like this and become involved in his or her life. Take that person out to lunch. Invite him or her to be a part of your small group.

Drop a line.

Text a Bible. (We're being serious.)

1 Text the word Bible to 20222. Wait for a confirmation text message.

2 Send the word YES.

3 That's it. You just sent a Bible to a persecuted Christian. You will get a $5 charge on your billing statement.

This mission is through Open Doors. For more information about this go to opendoorsusa.org.

Pen, say hello to paper.

20222

Lots of bullies on the playground.

More Christians have been persecuted in the last 100 years than in all of the previous 1900 years since the time of Christ. You might be surprised to know of persecution against Christians that happens close to home. Go to christianfreedom.org and search under United States, Mexico, or UK to inform yourself about persecution near to you.

Push a pencil.

180

IDOP. (You're thinking about pancakes right now, aren't you?)

Well, we are talking about something altogether different. Visit persecutedchurch.org and order a free IDOP (International Day of Prayer) kit. Use it to make your church aware of the needs of persecuted Christians around the world.

Save the ink industry. (Write things down.)

182

We're not the only ones.

Visit a local Islamic mosque and speak with an Imam (Islamic priest) about his experience with persecution in the United States.

White spaces are meant to be filled, says us.

Back to school.

Look up forums/lectures at a local university and attend one where the Christian worldview is in the minority.

Do tell.

Endnotes

1 Roger L. Hahn, *Matthew: A Commentary for Bible Students* (Indianapolis: Wesleyan Publishing House, 2007), 103.

2 Harold Ivan Smith, *A Decembered Grief: Living with Loss While Others Are Celebrating* (Kansas City: Beacon Hill Press, 1999).

3 Mike Crawford and his Secret Siblings, *Songs from Jacob's Well*, vol. 2, "Words to Build a Life on" (2008).

4 William Barclay, *New Testament Words* (Louisville, KY: Westminster John Knox Press 2000), 241.

5 Michael J. Wilkins, *The NIV Application Commentary* (Grand Rapids: Zondervan Publishing, 2004), 207.

6 Roger L. Hahn, Matthew: *A Commentary for Bible Students*, 103.

7 Michael J. Wilkins, *The NIV Application Commentary*, 209.

the kingdom experiment
YOUTH EDITION

thekingdomexperiment.com
twitter.com/KEyouth

the kingdom is backwards